Nothing But Yet

Nothing But Yet

How To Turn Your Mom Life Crisis
into Your Rebirth!

Tasha G.

Nothing But Yet

Copyright © 2026 by Latasha Snell-Gatling

Paperback ISBN: 978-1-971712-06-2
Ebook ISBN: 979-1-971712-07-9

Quill and Company Publishing

QuillandCompany.com
TheQuillandCompany@gmail.com

For Qiana —
My sister-friend,
my co-visionary,
my soft place to land.

You were one of the first to see me.
To trust me.
To say, "I'm ready" — and choose me to walk beside you
as you healed, built, dreamed, and dared.

You were more than a founding member of the Mom Maintenance
Community —
you were its heartbeat.
A believer in sisterhood, in evolving and becoming,
in showing up for women when the world tried to shut us down.

You gave me your time, your money, your faith —
not because you had to,
but because you believed I was *worth it*.
That I was *ready* to pour into you.
And Sis, your belief poured back into me
on days when I barely had a drop left for myself.

Your light was stolen far too soon
at the hands of violence you did not deserve.
But your legacy lives — in every page of this book,
in every woman who finally breathes again
because she remembered her worth.

This is for you, Q.
For your courage.
For your laugh.
For your love.
For your *Yet* that still echoes in us all.

I miss you every day.
And I carry you with every step forward.

**Forever your SisterFriend,
Tasha G.**

Foreword

I never expected an amusement park to be the place where I'd reach my breaking point. Yet, there I was on a hot summer afternoon feeling utterly invisible on what was supposed to be a fun family trip. The air smelled of funnel cake and fried chicken, kids were screaming with laughter on the roller coaster and my own children ran in front of me with my husband, eager for the next ride. On the surface I probably looked like any tired mom hustling after her family, but inside a storm was brewing. I had asked – practically begged – that we leave by 7:00 PM because we needed to find a place to have dinner and I was the designated driver for the two-hour drive home. I knew my limits: after a full day of navigating crowds, keeping everyone fed and happy, I could feel the exhaustion setting in. I just wanted to go home; to have a moment of peace for myself that evening. But as 7:00 came and went, my request went unheard.

I was so hurt watching my husband hurry to the next ride with the kids as if he didn't realize it was getting later and later. My spouse and kids kept finding "one more thing" to do. One more snack, one more ride, one more hour of waiting for them to be ready to leave. Nobody seemed to hear me. With each passing minute, as the sun dipped lower and my feet ached, a familiar feeling rose in my chest – that choking sensation of being dismissed and unheard, of being expected to give and give without question. I wanted to text my 2 girlfriends but figured they were tired of hearing this same sob story.

At that moment a lightbulb went off that seemed to be the perfect outlet. I texted myself my thoughts and in those three hours of my family having the time of their lives, I had the draft of this book. I texted my girlfriends to update them and shared the outline of my book and they could see the vision of it too. For the first time that evening I had a genuine smile on my face.

It was after 10:00 PM when we finally left the park—almost three hours after I had asked to go. I sat in silence behind the wheel, exhausted, not just physically, but emotionally. That moment wasn't really about the park. It was about years of feeling unheard. Years of putting myself last. Years of being everything for everyone else… while slowly disappearing in my own life.

I felt stuck – stuck in a cycle of being the "good mom" and "good wife" who never rocked the boat, even when I was drowning inside. I felt…empty. And that terrified me. I wrote everything – how angry I was that I didn't stand up for myself at the park, how guilty I felt for being angry, how I had this sudden clarity that the issue was so much bigger than one day's outing. I wrote that I felt like I didn't matter, that I was tired of being invisible. Somewhere in that outpouring, I found a glimmer of something I hadn't felt in a long time: self-worth. I realized that I was writing not just a diary entry – I was writing a promise. A promise to myself that something had to change, that I would find a way out of this crisis of the soul. That moment of writing was the first time I had really listened to my own voice in ages. It felt like striking a match in a pitch-black room; for the first time, I could begin to see the outlines of the walls trapping me, and I could imagine a door.

And in that moment, something shifted. That text to myself became the seed of the very book you're reading now. I didn't know it at the time – I was just trying to survive my feelings – but by dumping my heart onto those pages, I started a journey. I began creating the roadmap I desperately needed. Over the following months, whenever I felt that darkness creep in; there were many times, days when I felt like a failure. I recalled arguments where I lost my voice again, mornings I could barely get out of bed and I would return to the draft. My book manuscript became a place where I could be honest with myself. Slowly, pattern by pattern, I started to see what had brought me to that breaking point. And slowly, step by step, I began to climb out. This book is the culmination of that process – a process of reflection, healing, and transformation. I share my story here not because I have it all figured out (I'll be the first to admit I'm still a work in progress, still navigating my way through new challenges), but because I don't want any other mom to ever feel as alone and unheard as I felt that day at the amusement park.

If you've picked up this book, there's a chance you've felt some version of what I felt: that you're running on empty, that you've lost a piece of yourself in the endless shuffle of making others matter before yourself. Maybe you've had your own moment – maybe not as dramatic as crying by the Ferris Wheel, but a moment nonetheless – where you thought, "I can't live like this, something has to give." If you have, I want you to know that moment of despair can become your turning point. It might not feel like it now, but it is often when we are cracked open that the light can finally break in. My hope is that through the chapters ahead, and through the simple exercises and journal prompts I'll share, you'll start to hear your own voice again. That you'll honor your voice, nurture it, and let it guide you toward your own rebirth. Think of me as a friend who's a few steps ahead on the path, reaching back with a flashlight. I've been through the dark tunnel of a Mom Life Crisis, and I'm here to walk with you and shout encouragement as you find your way out. You are not alone in this anymore. Together, we're going to turn that feeling of "nothing" – like you have nothing left, nothing for yourself – into "nothing but yet," which means your story isn't over. There is so much "yet" to come.

On that fateful day, I thought I was just texting myself to soothe my broken spirit. In reality, I was charting a course. I was writing the first chapter of a new life – one where I am seen, heard, and fulfilled, not just as a mother or a wife, but as me. And if I can do it, trust me, you can too. So if you're ready, flip the page. Let's begin this journey together. It's time to turn your Mom Life Crisis into your rebirth.

– "Tasha" G., Author of Nothing But Yet (Your sister-friend on this journey)

Contents

Chapter 1

Welcome to the Mom Life Crisis

The goals I had to make my life better and prove others wrong about me turned into mental chains that weighed me down. The goals I set for my life were supposed to save me: Get married. Have children. Get a good job. I thought those things would fix everything. Instead, they became mental chains that weighed me down. Being married, having children and getting that "good city job" didn't solve all of the problems and trauma I was drowning in. Sure it was great motivation during my 20s and 30s when I was fueled by Survival mode, but by my 40s; feelings of exhaustion, overwhelm and sheer fear of life's next chapter hit like a ton of bricks. The absence of wiser women in my life to guide me added to my heavy emotional burden and I clung to hiding behind People Pleasing and perfectionism to make it through. For years I was ashamed, feeling like no one loved me out loud, as if I weren't good enough. If my own parents didn't show me love and emotional support doesn't that mean I'm not lovable?

How could I find what was wrong with me so I could fix it and get to at least loving myself a little more?

The Pandemic was the breaking point for me. The anxiety and toxic negative coping skills I relied on, up until then, became the noose around my neck that was slowly strangling me daily. My body was constantly tense. My mind never shut off. I cried in silence, trying to hold it together for everyone else while falling apart inside.

I was juggling everything—work, school, motherhood—and I felt completely out of control.

My routine consisted of a tightened chest and teeth grinding in my sleep. All of this while my children were soundly sleeping, feeling like I was their superhero. I knew my small world had me on edge, but how was the real world this much out of control too!?!? Six months into the shutdown in 2020 I finally had my mental break: realizing how scared and out of control I felt, the pressures of trying to succeed, pursuing a master's degree online full time, teleworking and homeschooling full time, spraying groceries with Lysol and sanitizing my family within an inch of their lives. I didn't see an end in sight with the "new normal" and I was so overwhelmed and stuck at the same time. I couldn't find words to express how I felt, and I honestly didn't feel like I had time to spend figuring out why I was feeling so badly. In life I hadn't found ways to express myself authentically and it felt like I was paying the price for avoiding my mental and emotional needs for so long. The worst part of it was I didn't think I deserved to figure out why I was feeling like crap even though I had made it my life's work to help others figure out their issues.

The responsibilities I had were compounding, making me feel like the eldest child in charge of the house while the mother was constantly away. This sparked a familiar sadness that I realized had been a part of me for decades and I just couldn't ignore it anymore with the world shut down. After weeks of avoiding my feelings Google came to the rescue, revealing that I was dealing with Childhood Emotional Neglect. ***(Dr. Jonice Webb is a good resource to learn more about CEN. I'll share her info later on in this book.)*** Finally finding the words that describe how I felt gave me so much power! It made my feelings so much more palpable, as if it was written on the wall so I could no longer ignore it. Being able to put into words how I felt with the backing of research from doctors and coaches gave me the courage to finally face the all-consuming sadness that had me in a chokehold…. And THIS is when my Mom Life Crisis was realized.

I didn't even know what to call what I was going through… so I did what we all do—I went to Google. What I found made everything click: "While "mom life crisis" is not a formal Oxford dictionary entry, the concept is frequently discussed in popular culture and psychology as a specific form of midlife crisis or identity transition triggered by motherhood. It often involves:

- Matrescence: The intense biological, psychological, and social changes a woman undergoes throughout motherhood.
- Identity Shift: Grappling with the loss of self, career stagnation, or the transition of children growing up.

- "Midlife Unraveling": A term sometimes used to describe the questioning of one's life direction.

Now the thing with my Mom Life Crisis is I didn't feel like I ever truly knew myself, so the disconnect I was experiencing was on a deeply personal level. Realizing pockets of my life were wiped from my mind as a trauma response sparked a fear in me to figure things out so I wouldn't feel like I lost anymore precious time. With three children growing up so fast I wanted to make sure I could remember those core memories we were building together. Could I continue to be ignorant when it comes to my emotions, constantly pouring into everyone so they can have the security and happiness I was craving? Did I finally have the courage to say enough is enough, take my power back, and stop allowing others in my life to drain me of my time, energy and peace, even when they didn't deserve it?

It felt like I started a different type of female cycle that I wasn't prepared for. I didn't know what I needed but I knew I had to figure it out fast. After working with personal and professional development coaches, watching hours of inspirational and motivational videos, listening to audio books and talking about my feelings with my trusted circle I felt even worse! (I knew you weren't expecting that!) I started to realize how much more I needed to do in order to find my peace and happiness and I was FREAKING EXHAUSTED! So, I did what I knew best: put my People Pleasing Pushover Hat back on and hoped I could keep myself distracted from the real work I needed to do to heal. I felt like I was smooth sailing, giving out personal and professional advice to dozens, watching them grow and find success with my guidance and support while I felt like I was barely treading water in my own life. Fast forward 2 years and now marital strife was at an all-time high. I thought I was a goner. Was my marriage of over 10 years going to be over? Was there even a relationship to save with the way things were going? Did we grow apart and I was too busy helping others to be aware of this? Was I being the "understanding wife" that didn't want to confront major issues happening for years that now backfired on me? Were other relationships in my life crashing and burning because I wasn't standing up for what was best for me?

This emotional spiral led to severe bouts of overthinking, depression and anxiety. Overthinking my daily moves, hoping I didn't make any costly mistakes that would cause me more grief and pain. Depression and shame from things in my past that I couldn't go back and change. And anxious about the future that seemed to be painfully unraveling, leaving me feeling out of control and my Type A personality was turning my mind and emotions into a powder keg, ready to explode at any given moment. I was holding on for dear life and it felt like I was failing at everything. A business coach I was working with told me the words I needed to hear but hated receiving: "LaTasha, my Word for you is you need to trust. That's what you need to work on this year." That was in Fall 2023. I leaned into it and thought, "Ehh, I'll get to it." But then God said, "Oh Sis, this is not to be done on your time, but on mine. So let me snag this little piece of rug from under you so you can see it's time for your Rebirth…" I thought I'd survived the worst, until late 2023 dealt me one more heavy blow – a layoff that snatched away my last sense of stability. I was displaced from work with 3 days notice, pushing me even deeper into my Mom Life Crisis.

After months of trying to find some semblance of normalcy so I could relax mentally and emotionally, I begrudgingly waved the white flag, realizing I had to REALLY rebuild, without a blueprint or plan in sight. My 20 years in the professional workforce did not seem to be pushing me in the right direction to get back on track financially. My marriage was hanging on by a thread (an interesting story for another time). I was reduced to taking underpaying driving jobs, and my family was transitioning into so many different chapters of their lives. I was LOSING IT! I started picking up bad habits that were not helping the process: making excuses for not going to the gym, binge-watching dozens of movies and doomscrolling until 3 AM; leading to me pulling all nighters for weeks on end because of the Pandemic. My uptake in eating sugary sweets (like a whole strawberry shortcake in a week alone) became my norm. At the time I didn't realize my anxiety was causing me to eat my feelings, and I had a LOT of feelings…

The triggers were triggering; jolting me back to my 6 year old self in South Carolina who was unexpectedly uprooted to the Bronx after losing my caregiver, my great grandmother, affectionately called Mama, to an unexpected heart attack. Losing Mama left an ache in my heart that's still there today, because I never got to say goodbye to her. She passed away in the hospital and I was too small to visit her. This was one of the first times I remember feeling unseen. I don't remember anyone asking me if I was ok or even if I wanted to see her or missed her. No one asked if I was heartbroken that the woman who raised me was ripped out of my life, or if I even understood what death was. I honestly thought no one truly cared… I couldn't go back to being that girl again; she had no power and was violated and traumatized by many. That little girl in me felt like she wasn't good enough to be a wife or mother because she hadn't been loved in a way that helped her find her confidence and true self. Instead she was forced into a position of feeling like her only survival was staying quiet and keeping other people's secrets while pretending everything was ok. Using humor and getting good grades in school for protection and external validation as a child, I had to figure out my life from nothing while holding onto my Insane Faith in the process… yeah, to learn to thrive I had to hold onto nothing but yet…

*****

If you are in your Mom Life Crisis I want to help make this realization more palatable for you. You still have to find ways to live and learn to love life, all while learning to love yourself. Even though it's scary, it's your time to learn to live by choice, not by chance. You don't have to wait for permission to choose yourself. Figuring out what you want in life will help you build the habit of setting boundaries with people who play in your face. If they don't love or respect themselves it means they won't love or respect you, and to keep it real, you are making it a cycle when you don't put yourself first. Choosing yourself is a luxurious act of self-love- something you actually deserve! I didn't have much help gathering myself and finding clear ways to think, regulate my emotions and prioritize my needs in life. To be honest, most of the time I'm exhausted because I've realized the toxic habits I'd been using to survive just aren't going to cut it in this chapter in my life. I am dealing with decisions I've made years ago that I still am obligated to and it saddens me that I ignored how broken I was for so long. I got tired of the hamster wheel of regret and self doubt I was on because it was keeping me from my potential. The way I had no consistency or discipline for things unless it was counterproductive was protruding like a pimple on a teen's face, getting me to the point of being tired of my own bad habits. Maybe it's a trauma response, but I found myself stuck in a mode of having to be literally sick of my own shit to change, like I'm a glutton for punishment. I've learned ways to turn my pain into purpose and I'm using that purpose to make clear actionable steps and exercises to help you on your personal growth journey. Shortening the learning curve for others is what we should do with our wisdom and life experiences. I know it hurts, but a lot of times that pain has a purpose that you just don't see right away; like how I started to become consistent so I could see progress in the bad times.

I knew I needed a way to process everything I was feeling in real time—not just survive it. This book will guide you through the four stages of my CASE (Cry, Assess, Supplement, Evaluate) framework that elevates your emotional awareness. This will lead into discussing the three buckets you need to work on for balance in your life, followed by a strategic, abundant PLAN for your life. The CASE framework helps you with processing and managing your pain and emotions in real time, while the three buckets help you determine how you, your loved ones and your career are affecting your current mental and emotional state. Then your PLAN will help you to get on track with better habits after you have come to a place of acceptance and are ready to do the work. It is ok if you did not realize you were settling in your life for love and respect from others that you give a lot to. Most of us don't realize this because we are happy with the breadcrumbs we receive so we feel needed and not alone. This is the time for you to accept that you were waiting for permission to determine what would make you happy in life. It's time to tune into what you won't stand for when dealing with others, and accept why you keep putting your dreams on hold waiting for someone else to give you permission to heal, thrive and demand more in life.

When you really think of it, you've been in **M.O.M. Mode**: Making Others Matter, robotically moving through life meeting everyone else's needs and putting them first, while you have been suffering mentally and emotionally because no one is pouring into you. Your go to outlets are extreme: silence and shutting down or being passive aggressive and acting like you don't need anyone for anything. After all of this anguish it's finally time for the change to come that you've been praying for. Let's make your CASE together! On a sheet of paper, in your notebook or on your phone answer these prompts:

- **Cry it out** (What emotions have you been holding in? Can you give yourself permission to feel them fully?)

This was difficult for me because when the pent up emotions started to unleash it made space for me to see how much disrespect I allowed from others because I was living through my trauma of craving love and/or companionship. Getting to know myself and being honest with what I really wanted helped me with building the habit of setting boundaries with myself. I had to really get tired of my lazy self care ways. I had to keep it real; I was scared of more change that would remind me of the things that are out of my control. Accepting negative attention in toxic situations with toxic people made me feel like I was taking lashes to the back then letting someone splash 91% isopropyl alcohol on afterwards while thanking them for it and letting them know they missed a spot. I had to keep in the forefront of my mind that I was being my worst nightmare, a glutton for punishment, making excuses for people harming me mentally and emotionally and not believing I was enough to make myself happy. Trust me, crying when the spirit moves you DEFINITELY helps!

TRY THIS: Write down one instance where you held back tears or pain. What do you think might have happened if you allowed yourself to cry it out?

- **A**ssess your situation (What is REALLY happening here that you can change??)

Crying allows you to make space for your awareness. Crying has been a hard emotion for me to manage because it makes me feel so freaking vulnerable. When I remember crying as a child it was because I felt really hurt or abandoned, leading to me feeling so alone and awkward. You can start the process by taking a good hard look at your situation. If you've been clinging to survival mode this is the time to start deactivating and regulating it. It's time to take accountability for your part in the way your life is set up and you need to stop the BLAME GAME. Yes people can do things that upset and hurt you that are out of your control, but what have YOU been doing? You can't expect others to keep it real with you and you're not being honest with yourself about how you've been feeling, and more importantly what you need. Part of being painfully steeped in the Mom Life Crisis is ignoring your needs and putting others before you. When you really think about that, what has existing in this way really done for you? Honestly, has it been more of a benefit or a drain? What is really happening right now that you can change to feel more empowered? Let's start with ways you can feel like you are really living life, not just existing.

TRY THIS: What's one specific area in your life where you feel stuck right now? Why's that?

- Supplement your emotional well-being (What do you need right now to help you feel better?)

Life has so many things happening everywhere all at once and it can be difficult to pinpoint where you need to focus attention at times. I didn't learn the importance of focusing on my own needs until the Pandemic made me take a long hard look at myself. I thought it would be selfish to think of myself and fill my own cup to my heart's content. Looking around at the women in my life I really didn't know one who did things for herself, and that was a crying shame. I had no idea where to start because of the sheer terror I felt leaving my children for my own alone time, the poverty mindset of spending money on just myself. Low self worth kept me entrenched in feeling like, "Since no one else appreciated my worth why should I?" I had to learn to treat myself like I would my best friend, giving myself grace, love and pep talks to motivate and inspire. This helped me be ok with not being ok so I could figure out what I needed at different times in my life, grounding me in so many ways. It also hurt me to think how no one else had put in this amount of effort for my mental and emotional well being before.

TRY THIS: Can you answer this: Do you currently have an impulsive emotional feeling that makes you anxious? What can you do within your control that could help keep you calm?

- Evaluate and plan your next steps.

This is one of the best parts of your healing journey because it's where your peace and freedom lies! You've been praying for a way to have your voice heard, your heart seen, and your mind celebrated for its beauty. Who better to do this than you? You have to PLAN for your next steps and really dream with no parameters. Take a deep breath because I know you thought you would NEVER get to this point; to think about yourself and truly realize it is paramount that you are important enough to live by choice, not by chance. You deserve this… you have survived 100% of the things you've gone through, right? And we are going to find a beautiful reason for this!

TRY THIS: Answer this question: How can I move forward positively from this moment in a way that benefits me?

Get yourself a cup of tea and a snack so we can get to work because there are solutions to your Mom Life Crisis and this book is going to provide you with that missing blueprint! Remember it's nothing but YET!

Now that you've identified what your Mom Life Crisis looks like… let's talk about one of the first things people tell you to do next. Alexa: Play Michael Jackson's You Are Not Alone!

*****

Chapter 2

Go to therapy they said…

Why Therapy?

"Go to therapy," they said. Like it was easy. Like it didn't require unpacking years of pain you barely had the language for. Therapy wasn't something I ran toward. It was something I avoided… until I couldn't anymore. With the Mom Life Crisis being about you making a decision that prioritizes your needs, therapy can be really helpful. Therapy is where you finally get to hear yourself. Not the version of you that shows up for everyone else…but the version of you that's been buried under survival mode. For me, therapy became the first place where my feelings weren't dismissed, rushed, or ignored. Life happens… you will deal with issues like depression, anxiety, stress, trauma, relationships and various other difficult life events in our heads and hearts. Well here's the kicker: most of these issues will impact you because of others you interact with in your life. The way you are interwoven into the fabric of others' lives by circumstance is amazing and overwhelming at the same time.

Therapy helped me to see how much of my unhealed past triggered my present situations. I grew up learning to silence myself. When chaos happened around me, I didn't process it—I absorbed it.And that silence followed me into adulthood, shaping how I showed up in relationships, in motherhood… and in my own life.

In those moments I learned to swallow my feelings and fear in silence, mistaking my need for emotional regulation as being too needy or a burden. I didn't realize moments like these were the links in the heavy chains that were weighing me down that I mentioned earlier.

Therapy helps you to work on self awareness, healthier communication, boundaries and those triggers that make up who you are and how you react. The work done in therapy is where the seeds of your REBIRTH are planted, cultivated and tailored to your needs. What you work on and pay attention to will grow, positive or negative. Looking at my family history there wasn't anyone I knew who went to therapy. When I first went in my 20s I wasted that poor young lady's time. Growing up I was taught "what happens in the house stays in the house…", and it took me a long time to shake that limiting belief. To be honest I still struggle with it, and during the Pandemic it suffocated me into a depression; I knew I needed to talk about it. At this time I found another therapist, a woman from the West Indies that told me, "Do you want me to agree with you or do you want me to keep it real with you?" I answered the latter but there was still no connection there. I didn't feel comfortable enough to let her into my truths, shame and fears. I had decades of pent up mental and emotional PTSD that had become the bullets loaded into my Mom Life Crisis gun, with the Pandemic being the trigger that erratically started going off. Each session I sat there stiff as a board, wanting to spill everything but terrified of what would happen if I opened that floodgate. My tongue felt glued to the roof of my mouth – years of not talking doesn't unravel easily.

Unconventional Coping

When therapy didn't work the first time, I thought something was wrong with me. But the truth was—I wasn't ready yet. I realized my pent-up feelings were like a soda bottle I'd been shaking for years – no wonder I exploded when life got rough and out of my control. Talking released some of that pressure. Because I wasn't emotionally or mentally supported growing up I had zero preparation when it came to talking about my feelings and the toxic situations and people that were suffocating me. This was a major reason the round of therapy didn't work out in 2020. I started using social media to share what I was feeling and it actually started to help me. Though unconventional it was nice to talk through my feelings online and have engagement from those it resonated with. I even connected with some people who I talked with offline and those bonds helped me through a lot of the turmoil I was drowning in.

I was shocked that talking, the thing I was told not to do, was actually the thing I needed to help me feel better. Talk therapy is a form of treatment that involves discussing thoughts, feelings and behaviors. It empowers you by providing a supportive environment that you can make safe, where you can have open and honest communication to come up with a treatment plan of goals and strategies. Now at the time I didn't think social media was going to help me in the ways it did, but I'm glad I chose to open up and talk. This led me to attracting others who resonated with me, including my dear friend Qiana whose life was tragically taken due to domestic violence in 2025.

Losing Qiana gutted me; it was a stark reminder of how crucial this inner work is – sometimes it's literally life or death. She became my first paying client when I embraced becoming a Mindset and Wellness Coach. When I started working with Qiana I looked in the mirror and said out loud, 'You see, little Tasha? We did it, and we deserve this success!' I didn't realize at the time the rough coals of my past I'd been carrying around for so long, were being pressurized and formed into the diamond gems that would change not only my life, but the lives of so many others who were struggling in their Mom Life Crisis.

Facing the Ultimate Test

They say third times a charm, so when I went back into therapy in 2024 I decided I would really open up to make the most out of the experience. I walked into that third therapist's office with my heart in my throat but a strange steely resolve in my gut – I knew this was do-or-die for me emotionally. I was done holding back. By this time more of life started crumbling on top of me. I was primarily driving for work, putting a lot of stress on myself and my vehicle, and my husband and I were in a bad space. Then everything shifted. My husband told me he needed space—not just emotionally, but physically… and relationally. He wanted freedom to explore connections with other women. And just like that, the foundation I thought I was standing on cracked beneath me. He wanted the power of choice in his life which was something that was taken from him because of his own traumatic past. I was in shock. Not just as a wife—but as a woman who had spent years trying to be enough. It triggered something deeper than the moment. It took me back to every time I felt unseen, unchosen, and not enough.

I remember my hands trembling as he spoke, my heart breaking into tiny pieces, and strangely not even able to cry at first. It wasn't just wife-me that felt discarded – it was little-girl-me all over again, feeling 'not good enough' for someone to stay. It took months before the truth came out about his Lethario ways. At that time I was super triggered, wanting to talk to him about the fate of our relationship, but he only gave emotional and physical unavailability, spending nights out and leaving me alone and stuck with more questions than answers. I couldn't believe that I was in a place of knowing the love of my life, my partner, was actively "spending time" with other people while I sat at home with all of the responsibilities and feeling like I must've done something wrong in order to be treated this way. Migraines and acid reflux became a by-product of the stress and worry I was dealing with. A familiar trauma response engulfed me during this time. My hands and feet were freezing cold, as if blood was not circulating to those parts, my mind was on a constant loop thinking of him being with various women while treating me like a roommate. I would then be confused with him by coming back and being loving and caring a few days a week. My nervous system was so dysregulated I don't think I would've made it through without having my trusted circle of friends supporting me.

I was in shock. Not just as a wife—but as a woman who had spent years trying to be enough. It triggered something deeper than the moment. It took me back to every time I felt unseen, unchosen, and not enough. I was at a point of exhaustion myself, dealing with so many situations that were out of my control and not feeling like I had a say in how my own life should go. I wanted my marriage and my family. I knew my husband and I loved each other and being with our children, but I did not feel comfortable knowing I was being disrespected by someone who was supposed to make me feel safe. I didn't have an outlet to recharge and his mid life crisis compounded my Mom Life Crisis, triggering feelings of low self worth and lack of boundaries. I felt like I was being kicked when I was already down because I was still looking for better work and the fear of not being able to take care of my family by myself was daunting. That didn't mean my husband wasn't still providing, but with so much confusion and uncertainty in our relationship I didn't feel secure not standing on my own two feet financially so if and when he changed his mind I'd have my own back.

I understood we all go through things, so my husband experiencing his own PTSD was not something I didn't believe could happen, however I didn't have to agree with the way I was being disrespected, neglected and mistreated. This "rough patch" as my husband called it, made me feel like I was a child again, dealing with my mother who was emotionally unavailable and I was sick of it. I spoke up for myself, letting it be known how uncomfortable I felt, but trying to get him to see my perspective was difficult because he was in a selfish zone. While I was trying to heal myself, my marriage was unraveling. I was leaning closer and closer to divorce when he said I still hadn't made a therapy appointment after him mentioning it a few times. I was still working through the grief of the situation and was ready to hand in the towel.

My husband was stuck in his mindset, bringing more hurt and pain into my life and I was craving peace so I would just think. I should've been prepared that my husband may not have been ready to truly commit to the work therapy called for that could help us repair our relationship. And then my therapist asked me a question that stopped me in my tracks: "It sounds like your husband wants to have control of something in his life after feeling out of control for so long. What do you want?" I can't lie, this was hard for me to answer. I wanted my family. I wanted to have a husband that loved and respected me out loud and I had to accept that this was not the case. Instead I was in a situation that made me feel like I was being held under water with hands wrapped around my neck firmly applying pressure to my windpipe in an effort to make me concede.

Setting Boundaries/ Choosing Yourself

This round of therapy showed me that I was waiting for someone to choose me, and the person was not my husband, but myself. I needed to choose me! Therapy felt like a luxury I didn't deserve – but that was a lie. Emotional well-being isn't a luxury; it's a necessity. In fact, it's the ultimate luxury to finally treat yourself like you matter. Almost a year went by before I got back into therapy again. The reason for going back was because I voiced I was exhausted and done with the marriage, ready to submit the divorce papers for real this time, which was met with, "I mentioned therapy three times and you haven't made an appointment." *insert eye roll here*. To be completely transparent, my husband had done too much to me. It was a losing battle because we weren't at a point where the apology was as loud as the disrespect. In the process of going through marital strife I found myself and after many grieving nights I embraced that I deserved better not only from him, but from myself.

Amid the heartbreak, I had an unexpected moment of peace – I realized this upheaval was forcing me to finally put *me* first. It was terrifying, but also liberating, like feeling the sun on your face after a long time underground. This time therapy would be for working on better communication because we would still be in each others' lives for co-parenting. I was ready to choose self respect regardless of his actions. It took some time to work on triggers, but my emotional regulation was worth so much more than being insecure and upset over things I couldn't control. I did the bucket exercise and came to terms with the fact that I was being drained by someone who was straddling the fence and relying on the love and the history we had to drag me and walk all over me. At the time of me writing this we only had one session where the feedback from the therapist was to work on myself and choose what I wanted and needed. Even though it's been hard I've been embracing this time in my life that's really about me. I came to the conclusion that in my life I have taken care of everyone more than myself; in committed relationships for almost 20 years, a mom for over 18 years, a devoted friend to many for decades.

The Mom Life Crisis I was going through was resetting my internal compass to chart a course I didn't know I needed to take. I had to accept the fact that I was building a future with someone who was not on the same page. It seemed difficult for us to communicate, so I was relieved when my husband mentioned going to therapy. I made an appointment for two weeks away and I worked on getting my words together to present to the therapist. I wanted to finally be heard by my husband after all these years, and not being seen as badgering or threatening. I wanted him to see my side in our relationship: how feeling like he had control of how much of himself he would give to me even though he swore he loved me left me feeling empty. How even though he steadily proclaimed he was still in love with me I was hurt from his lies, deceit and betrayal of my trust.

We both showed up to the first session in different spaces of our home, something that was highlighted by the therapist in the first 30 seconds. The level of disconnect we were experiencing was nauseating because I felt my husband was controlling the situation and wanted to keep us in a bad space because he was adamant about getting his way. I felt like he wanted my permission to cheat and I was setting boundaries on how uncomfortable the situation made me feel, which he didn't like. Of course the therapy session was met with his fixed mindset and we got nowhere fast. The blessing was I was back in therapy and sticking to it for myself. Sometimes people are in your life to push you to be greater when you may not have been able to do it for yourself. Of course this story is to be continued. Maybe I'll write another book about it!

Does this resonate with you? Have you been going through such chaos that you didn't even realize you've been flapping in the wind all this time in different important aspects of your life? Have you been afraid to take charge because it's been hard to put yourself first? Well you're not alone in feeling this way, going through this, or healing through this. Therapy has been something I didn't know I needed and didn't realize by talking, which was something I enjoyed, could heal deep wounds that were so old they triggered new ones so easily. I was SUCH a mess! I've decided to choose myself first and foremost, setting boundaries so I can truly go after what I needed, wanted and deserved in life. The crazy part is you really don't know how hard this was for me. Through therapy I had to embarrassingly embrace what I was allowing in my life that was indeed causing my unhappiness. This is where the bucket exercise really helped me see that love was not enough to give me the security and stability I deserved and needed to escape out of the survival mode that had been my evil companion for so long.

Therapy helped me to see that others were triggering me because I wasn't giving myself the grace to process my pain and disappointment. It was like keeping my foot in the door of a closing subway train hoping what I wanted would enter instead of embracing what I needed to cut off so I could heal. Being able to talk through my feelings while receiving validation for being uncomfortable and wanting better for myself was the confirmation I needed. After waiting for the love, structure and stability of my parents who were physically and emotionally unavailable, then getting into relationships, platonic and intimate, that left me lacking in the same way, I had to embrace the exhaustion I was experiencing. It was a sign that I had to figure out how to take my power back. If I didn't think I was worthy of my own love why would anyone else want it or even cherish it? If I couldn't be what I wanted or needed in my life how could I expect a certain standard from others?

Having a therapist to not only hear me but help me focus on ways that guided me out of the dark opened my eyes to accepting what I've allowed out of fear for countless years that made me feel unappreciated, unseen and unheard in my life. If what I've discussed resonates with you, I mean really hits that spot in your soul that's been aching for validation and peace, check out these tips to help you get started with therapy. And remember, it's up to you to make the choice that suits your life. If you're thinking about therapy but don't know where to start, here's what I learned the hard way:

- *Research therapists who specialize in Cognitive Behavioral Therapy or Emotionally Focused Therapy, for starters to see which one speaks to your situation.*

- *Ask for a free consultation to test the rapport and energy of the therapists you find. Date before you commit!*
- *If traditional talk therapy doesn't click, consider alternatives (group therapy, trauma-focused therapy, etc.,).*
- *If access or cost is an issue, look into community support groups or online therapy options.*

Journaling Prompt

1. **What sayings or 'rules' did you learn growing up that might be holding you back from seeking help or expressing yourself now?**

2. **Write down at least one, and then challenge it – is it really true or helpful for you today?**

Of course coming up with a Plan can be scary, but isn't it scary hoping people will do what you want them to do to make you feel loved and appreciated? Aren't you tired of living by chance and not by choice? The fastest way to correct this mindset is by creating new habits that prioritize your needs unapologetically and give you back your power. Choosing to turn your Mom Life Crisis into your Rebirth makes the space for a Plan that affirms your worth, value and future. Imagine being able to manage those anxious feelings of looking for love and validation in all the wrong places because you can confidently give it to yourself? Why continue the vicious cycle of HOPING someone sees and loves you when you can see and love yourself? I'm talking about taking yourself on solo dates to eat what you like, or going to see the movie you've been waiting to be released… or how about taking a 3 day trip and letting someone else figure out how to get the kids around so you can truly relax! I know this sounds damn near impossible but you're worth taking the first step by considering therapy and finding out who you are and who you want to become. One thing that kept me from drowning was making voice notes on my phone just to release what I was feeling – kind of like my own mini therapy session when no one was around. If you're not ready for a therapist, try recording or writing out your uncensored thoughts for 5 minutes a day.

My happiness is tied to helping others like me, who need support and guidance, self awareness and accountability through the chaotic confusion we call life; a light through the pain and transformation that comes in this new chapter that is all about you. Not only have I been able to process grief and pain better, I've also embraced that I am indeed in charge of my own life. When I take someone else's excuses and fear for living as a distraction I'm allowing them to trigger me into MOM Mode, Making Others Matter, causing me to forget myself and my needs. Setting boundaries to protect my time and energy is where my focus needs to be so I can not only embrace the changes I'm going through, I can prioritize my very own existence, giving myself an opportunity to feel, love and just be! Give yourself permission to heal, maybe even giving therapy a chance, and setting those much-needed boundaries. I'm still going through this process and it's not easy but I'm worth my effort! I hope you've learned from this chapter that choosing yourself isn't selfish; it's necessary. Now, let's turn these insights into personal action with some Mom Maintenance here. Grab your journal and reflect on the following:

- ***Think of a time you hid your true feelings.*** Maybe you held back tears or said "I'm fine" when you really weren't. Write about what happened and how it felt to keep those emotions inside. What might have been different if you had allowed yourself to express what you truly felt?

- ***Ask yourself what "choosing you" looks like.*** What is one decision or action you've been putting off that would make you feel cared for or recharged? Describe how taking that step (however small – whether it's scheduling a therapy session, carving out me time, or saying "no" to something draining) will benefit you and why you deserve it.

- ***Identify one boundary you need to set.*** It could be something like not answering work emails after dinner, or asking your family to help more with chores. Why is this boundary important for your well-being? Write down how you will kindly but firmly communicate this need to the people involved, and how you imagine life will feel once it's respected. Remember: every time you write and reflect, you're choosing yourself and taking a step toward your rebirth. And this book is your personal workbook – come back to these pages whenever you need a reminder that you matter, and to see just how far you've come.

They said 'go to therapy' as if it were easy – it wasn't. But it was worth it. In learning to speak my truth and put myself first, I found the key to the rebirth I desperately needed. Therapy was just the beginning… because what I discovered next changed everything. With that being said, Alexa Play Cardi B Get Up 10! – because this mama was down, but never out.

Chapter 3

Get Married and Have Kids They Said...

Now let's talk about another thing we were told would make everything better...

"Get married."

 "Have kids."

"Build a family."

They said it like it would complete me. Like it would fill every void I had been carrying since childhood. So I believed them. Not having emotional support growing up put me in survival mode and led me down a path of toxic and negative coping in situations and relationships. This is how my void was created. I remember so many times betraying myself trying to make others happy and being pulled in so many directions because of the judgement from others, leaving me in a place of insecurity and doubt. I used to feel like I had to be helping a person in some way in order to be in their presence.

Was there a time you stayed up all night helping a friend or relative who never thanked you? Or a moment you swallowed your own needs to please someone else and felt sick about it?

I remember bending over backwards for people because I wanted them to like me and I'm so nauseated by those memories… Being stuck waiting on a "friend" who didn't respect my time so they dragged their ass while I let someone I cared about down by being late because I wanted to avoid confrontation. I became the person who gave everything. My time. My energy. My attention. Not because I had it to give… but because I thought it was the price of being loved. After some time I started feeling like I had no one who truly loved me, so growing my family became a priority to fill that void. I wasn't the little girl who dreamt of the white wedding, pulling a pillow case over my head preparing for the day when I said, "I do…". Instead my thoughts were of having a baby shower where people would show how much they cared about me with fun and games in the packed event space, laughter and showering me with gifts.

I truly started believing I would have to give birth to the person who would truly love me. I vividly remember following the top baby brands to see what new must-have items were available so I would be prepared when I finally got a positive pregnancy test. From car seats to clothing I had an ongoing list I updated frequently in my brain as I watched others around me get pregnant and grow their families.   I literally craved that idea of love and validation that would come as a mother and prayed it would happen for me one day. I dreamed about becoming a mother. Not for the title—but for the love I thought it would bring. But even then, reality didn't match the dream. I went into early labor and missed both of my baby showers for my firstborn. Instead of being celebrated, I was in a hospital bed... watching it all happen without me. That's when I realized something wasn't adding up. I had built the life I thought I was supposed to want... but I still felt empty. I needed a way to understand why. That's when I created something that changed everything for me. I call it the **Three Buckets of Balance**. Because your life isn't just one thing—it's three:

- Yourself
- Your loved ones
- Your Career/ Calling

I've come up with this exercise on my personal growth journey and feel it will help so many visualize, become aware and willing to work on their mindset. Picture this: you are holding these buckets at all times in life. The bucket for You is on top of your head, with Loved Ones and Your Career/ Calling buckets in each hand. If any of these buckets are empty enough to be unbalanced it throws off your mood, energy, habits, perspective, and motivation. The goal isn't to get all of the buckets to be full all of the time, but to become aware of which bucket needs your attention. This is so you feel good about the effort it took to work to maintain a balance you're content with. Let's look at how these life buckets work:

- ***You*-** When your "You" bucket is full, you feel energized, confident, and present. When it's empty everything feels harder. You're exhausted, overwhelmed, and just trying to survive. I know you've probably been waiting for your knight in shining armor to come through and give you that soft place to land and you're borderline furious it hasn't happened yet. Instead you've battled through abuse, neglect, suffering, confusion, pain and God knows what else, feeling like you've been forgotten about. You can't keep going on like this! It's time to become aware of what's really happening in your life… all of it. The key to your thriving is that you have to be the one to choose and place yourself in place for your Rebirth intentionally. Your mindset is your prison or your paradise. The thoughts you live with daily shape your future, so if you think negatively and unkindly of yourself you will continue to live negatively. It's one of the worst habits you can create that's very hard to shake. When I first did this Bucket Exercise I realized my 'You' bucket was at a mere 3/10 – no wonder I felt drained! My Loved Ones bucket was a 7/10 and my Calling was around 5/10. That visual hit me hard, but it also gave me a starting point. Your goal is to find ways to give you what you need in a healthy way that is positive and empowering, and to set boundaries because your responsibility is to take care of yourself. Allow people to have the responsibility of taking care of themselves and if they need support or guidance they can reach out to you. Choose to value your time and energy and others will learn to do the same.

- ***Your loved ones*-** When this bucket is balanced, your relationships feel supportive and connected. When it's not, you feel drained, frustrated, and unseen… even by the people you love most. Does this sound familiar? Maybe you've felt that short fuse with your kids or partner when you're stretched thin. I don't know about you but I have felt tested by being around loved ones because they require so much of my time and energy. The Loved Ones bucket is almost as difficult to balance as the Yourself bucket because you need to learn the critical habit of confidently setting boundaries to show others how much you care about yourself first. We know people can get offended with boundaries, even if that was not your intention because their focus can be selfish. You don't have time or energy to constantly care for others at your own detriment, especially when you feel disrespected, unseen and unheard. Here's a question to ask yourself when determining how to manage the Loved Ones Bucket:

- How much time/ energy do I have to give to __________?
- If I'm feeling depleted would it make a difference to explain how I'm feeling? Why or why not?

- *Your Career/Calling*- This bucket reflects your purpose, growth, and financial stability. When it's off, you feel stuck, underpaid, or disconnected from who you're meant to be. For most of my life I felt this bucket was pretty full because I had a job and went to school for a few degrees. Yes, I said a few: 1 Associates, 1 Bachelors, 1 Masters with another one loading. I did get promotions at work, but after a few years I felt boxed in because it was not what I truly wanted. When I shifted my mindset because of this awareness my dreams started coming true and I was so scared. I always wanted the work/life balance I saw so many with, and it was good until it wasn't.

When I was displaced in 2023 I had to really look at my situation. With less than a week's notice my life took a turn, zooming into the unrecognizable, and I realized I was not as happy as I thought.

I went from a career of helping people to a career of looking for a job. After countless interviews with organizations I thought would lead to great opportunities I was reduced to driving jobs that were draining me mentally and physically. I hated keeping up the strong woman persona through it all, but I knew I didn't have a choice. I didn't want my children to see how bad things had gotten so quickly and I didn't want my husband to feel the pressure of the situation. I was wondering why God was testing me this way. I'd been working since I was 16 and this was not something I was used to. I felt ashamed and embarrassed that I was not able to make a good comeback, especially with my degrees and experience. By 2025 I felt like I was begging for a job that would honor my worth but the only ones willing to give me a chance were delivery jobs, leading to my car constantly having issues, putting an even bigger financial strain on my household. I prayed things would take a good turn and 2025 started out with me finally landing a job that paid well, but was demanding. The work/life balance I coveted was slowly slipping away pushing me to once again abandon my dreams for my responsibilities. I wanted to take the power back in my life by at least being able to provide for my family since my husband wanted out, so I was willing to give up some of my dreams yet again for my family.

I was so uncomfortable in my own skin and didn't think I would be able to survive one more thing going wrong. After a month of juggling the chaotic landscape of work with the duties of a stay at home mom I was dealt another blow. With no notice or good reason my services were no longer needed with no notice. Just when I thought I'd regained stability with a good job, the rug was pulled out from under me *again* – and it hit our family like a tsunami. Being unemployed twice in one year must've happened for a reason, right? I felt like God was telling me it was time to work on my purpose, my true calling, though I was scared and lost on how to really be successful at it. The only way to achieve that balance was to be honest with myself, work hard, and show up for myself the way I've done for countless others. But I'll tell you the mindset had me feeling like Superman holding Kryptonite in hand while trying to save the world. Why was so much on me?

I loved being a mother, but the responsibilities of motherhood were suffocating and there seemed to never be a break because the bills don't stop. Honestly, being a wife was not on my Bingo card. I always wanted to be a mother and was kind of obsessed with learning how to be a good one, but becoming a spouse was altogether different. My husband was the only man I thought I would marry because of our connection and the way God put us together. It just seemed right until it didn't. With his unhealed and unresolved traumas bursting like an infected cyst it really shook up our relationship. I could tell you how I feel about all of the things he's done that I know about and some of the things I have yet to find out, but his quest to find himself is not my focus. What I had to do was grow up and honestly look at the situation. I had to become aware that my low self worth put me into a position with him that caused me to allow a lot of disrespect, mistreatment, confusion and games to play out when I should've chosen me. I know a lot of you can relate to that feeling of wanting to save your family and not have your children seeing tension between their parents, but you deserve to choose you! I had to take accountability for the way I doubted myself over the years, thinking I would not be able to bloom in the way I saw myself in my wildest dreams because my current circumstances were so painful. It was time to face my fears, believe in myself, and not look back.

They said marriage and kids would complete me – they were wrong. I say taking care of *me* completes me. It took some time because I was letting go of the future I planned for my entire family, but the beauty is that I can build a new future for myself. It took me decades to realize that the emptiness I felt wasn't just about not having a husband or kids – it was about imbalance in what I now call my three life buckets. The world wasn't over, just one of the multiverses had come to an end. Facing this reality helped me heal more childhood wounds and put myself in a place to be proud of my growth. I was at the pivotal point in my life where I needed to live and love by choice, not by chance: it was nothing but YET!

Let's step into the Refill Zone…

Nothing But Balance: The Refill Zone: The Bucket Balance Assessment

Alright, let's see where your life is out of whack.

1. **Yourself**

2. **Your loved ones**

3. **Your career/calling**

Get your pen and journal- we're doing this together.

Balance Exercise 1

Goal: Let's create a quick visual of how balanced your life feels right now...

Instructions:

Current Fill Level: For each bucket, consider how "full" it feels right now, on a scale of 1 to 10 (where 1 is nearly empty and 10 is overflowing). Be honest with yourself. There are no right or wrong answers.

- **Yourself Bucket (Energy & Well-being):** How energized and well-cared for do you feel physically, mentally, and emotionally? (Score: ___)

- **Loved Ones Bucket (Relationships):** How healthy, fulfilling, and connected do you feel in your key relationships (partner, children, family, close friends)? (Score: ___)

- **Career/ Calling (Purpose & Growth):** How satisfied, challenged, and aligned do you feel with your work, career aspirations, or learning goals? (Score: ___)

1. **Visual Representation (Optional but Recommended):**

    - **Drawing:** On a piece of paper, draw three circles or rectangles representing your buckets. Shade in each bucket according to your score (e.g., 5/10 would be half-filled).

    - **Jars and Beans:** If you prefer a more tactile approach, find three jars and some beans or small objects. Assign each jar to a bucket and fill it with beans according to your score.

2. Reflect on the Visual: Look at your visual representation.

- Are the buckets relatively even in their fill level?
- Is one or more buckets significantly lower than the others?
- Is any bucket feeling like it's overflowing, contributing to your happiness, or is it closer to empty, causing strain?

Journaling Prompts

Answer the following questions in your journal. Take your time and use the questions as they make sense to your current situation. Remember this is you taking the time to embrace your Rebirth!:

- *Which bucket feels the most empty right now? What are some specific reasons for this?*
- *Which bucket feels the most full or even overflowing? Is this a healthy overflow, or is it draining other areas of your life?*
- *How does the imbalance (or balance) of these buckets affect your overall mood, energy levels, and motivation?*
- *What immediate feelings arise as you look at your bucket balance? (e.g., guilt, sadness, determination)*
- *Write out what you wish you could tell your family when you need time for yourself. Get all the honesty on paper.*

Balance Exercise 2

Identifying Drainers and Fillers

Goal: To pinpoint specific activities, relationships, and responsibilities that either deplete or replenish each bucket.

Instructions:

1. **Create Three Columns:** Now grab your journal and make three columns labeled "You," "Loved Ones," and "Career/Calling."

2. **Brainstorm Drainers:** For each bucket, brainstorm a list of things that currently drain your energy, time, or emotional resources in that area. Be specific.

   - **"You" Drainers:** (e.g., Lack of sleep, skipping meals, constant self-criticism, not having any alone time, neglecting hobbies)

   - **"Loved Ones" Drainers:** (e.g., Constant arguments with partner, feeling like you're the only one initiating connection, unresolved family conflicts, taking on everyone else's problems)

   - **"Career/Calling" Drainers:** (e.g., Overwhelming workload, feeling unappreciated at work, lack of clear goals, procrastination on studies, toxic work environment)

3. **Brainstorm Fillers:** For each bucket, brainstorm a list of things that bring you joy, energy, satisfaction, or a sense of

well-being in that area. Again, be specific.

- **"You" Fillers:** (e.g., Getting 6-8 hours of sleep, eating nutritious meals, going for a walk, reading a book for pleasure, practicing a hobby, quiet meditation)

- **"Loved Ones" Fillers:** (e.g., Meaningful conversations with your partner, playing with your children, spending quality time with friends, family dinners, expressing appreciation)

- **"Career/Calling" Fillers:** (e.g., Completing a challenging project, receiving positive feedback, learning a new skill, feeling a sense of purpose in your work, achieving academic goals, applying for a promotion you really want.)

4. **Analyze Your Lists:** Review your lists of drainers and fillers for each bucket.

- Are there more drainers than fillers in any particular bucket?

- Are there any drainers that you have direct control over changing or reducing?

- Are there any fillers that you can intentionally incorporate more of into your daily or weekly routine to motivate the building of new habits?

Journaling Prompts

Answer the following questions:

- What are the top 2-3 drainers in each bucket that have the biggest negative impact on you?

- What are the top 2-3 fillers in each bucket that bring you the most joy and energy?

- Are there any patterns you notice in your drainers or fillers across different buckets? (e.g., Do you tend to prioritize others' needs over your own in both the "Loved Ones" and "Career/ Calling" buckets? Have you been constantly putting off applying for promotions or going back to school?)

Balance Exercise 3

Identifying Areas for Change (The "One Small Step" Approach)

Goal: To move from awareness to identifying concrete, manageable steps for refilling and balancing your buckets.

Instructions:

1. **Focus on One Bucket:** Choose the bucket that feels the most empty or unbalanced in Balance Exercise 1.

2. **Review Your Drainers and Fillers:** Look at the lists you created in Balance Exercise 2 for that specific bucket.

3. **Identify Controllable Drainers:** Pick one or two drainers from that bucket that you have some level of control over reducing or eliminating.

4. **Brainstorm Small Steps:** For each chosen drainer, brainstorm 1-3 very small, specific, and achievable actions you could take this week to lessen its impact.

   - **Instead of:** "I need to get more sleep." **Try:** "Tonight, I will go to bed 15 minutes earlier than usual."
   - **Instead of:** "I need to stop arguing with my partner."

Try: "This week, during one disagreement, I will consciously take three deep breaths before responding."

5. **Identify Potential Fillers:** Pick one or two fillers from that bucket that you can realistically incorporate into your routine this week.

6. **Plan Specific Actions:** For each chosen filler, plan a specific time and way you will incorporate it.

   - **Instead of:** "I need to relax more." **Try:** "On Tuesday evening after the kids are in bed, I will take a 20-minute bath."

   - **Instead of:** "I need to connect with friends." **Try:** "I will send a text message to one friend on Monday to schedule a quick phone call this week."

Journaling Prompts

Answer the following:

- What is one small, specific step you can take this week to reduce a major drainer in your chosen bucket?

- What is one small, specific way you can incorporate a filler into your week for your chosen bucket?

- What potential obstacles might you encounter in taking these small steps, and how can you prepare for them?

- How will taking these small steps make you feel, even if it's just a little bit?

How did that feel? Eye-opening, I bet!

Good work – awareness is the first step! It's ok to not be ok with the Disney fairytale you thought your life was going to be. In the next chapter, we'll tackle that other piece many of us have been told will make us happy: your career/ calling. There's still time to create your Happily Ever After… it's Nothing But Yet… Now that you understand your balance… let's talk about what happens when your career doesn't align.

Alexa, Play Mary J. Blige "Just Fine"!

Chapter 4

Get a good job they said…

"Get a good job and you'll be set." That's what I was told. So I did exactly that. And for a while, it worked. Until it didn't. I followed the blueprint. I got the job. I built stability. I did everything I was told would lead to success. But deep down… I wasn't fulfilled. When I look back, I realize many of my career choices weren't mine. They were shaped by expectations… by pressure… by the need to prove myself. I wasn't building a life I wanted. I was building a life I thought I was supposed to live. I started a "Good City Job" and got my first apartment in 2004. I was so excited about taking the advice of others because I had no clue of the direction I needed to head in as a 24 year old woman. I was finally feeling like I was getting guidance from people in my life that wanted to see me succeed. I worked that job and gave birth to my son in 2006, becoming a single mother soon after. I was fortunate enough to have support from my son's grandparents which was a God send. That good Ole survival mode came out, pushing me forward to take care of myself and this little human being that really depended on me. Thanks to my son's grandmother I got that "Good City Job" along with support I always wished I'd gotten from my own family, and I'm forever grateful to her.

The one good thing about that "Good City Job" was the people there who supported me through being a young mother. I look back on it now and realize their wisdom, lived experience and perseverance made them want to help me through the choices I was making. One co-worker understood my journey all too well, being the mother of 5 "stairstep" children. She had her "Good City Job" for almost 2 decades and she was the matriarch of her family, battling through her own Mom Life Crisis. As the years of motherhood went by she shared what she went through with me, and now in my 40s her experiences really resonate with me. I thought I was making good choices based on the advice of others but when I look back at it, if I would've done what I wanted my career path would've been totally different. Getting a "Good City Job" was someone else's dream I followed, the same way some of you have become doctors, lawyers, nurses and teachers because of that nagging People Pleasing Pushover Hat we love to wear and hide behind. That's why the Career/Calling Bucket becomes so important in your journey. It gives you the opportunity to really dream about your life and if you want to get a degree or become a pilot. Would you rather be a daycare owner or a realtor? What about a butcher, a baker or a candlestick maker? See what I did there? LOL. Take your time and really think about this: some of you became teen moms, single moms, adoptive moms, or even geriatric moms (I hate that term!), which pushed your plans all the way off the board, replacing them with heavy family responsibilities.

You tasked yourself with wanting to make sure everyone is safe and secure, meanwhile you feel like you're dying inside. It's such a lonely, humbling place to be and my heart goes out to all of us that have been there, are there and will get there. Sometimes the career/calling path leads to a dead end when mixed with other things you have going on in life and it's ok to start over.

> **Reflection:** *Think back to your own career choices. Who were you trying to please or impress? Write down whose voice you hear in your head when you make decisions about your work or ambitions. Is it yours, or someone else's?*

In 2017 I left my "Good City Job" in NYC because God placed the thought in my mind back in 2013 to move to Maryland, and even though things got rough I still have faith that this was the best decision for my family. I'm crossing my fingers that it was the best decision for me too. I moved to Maryland for another "Good City Job". That leap of faith to leave a place I'd lived for 30 years for a chance at *more* – more growth, more income, more happiness – was me stepping into an abundance mindset, even if I didn't know the term back then. I had the belief that my aspirations would bear fruit. I didn't count on the shit that was also a part of the plan- but I take it as the fertilizer that was needed to help me transform and transcend into my Rebirth. I switched to a remote job opportunity in February 2021 that was great. It gave me the opportunity to be home with my children at one of the most uncertain times in our lives, only to be displaced November 2023. I struggled for years only being able to get driving jobs that didn't even provide me with half of the income I was accustomed to, putting a major strain on my family. The Pandemic and the Mom Life Crisis happening in tandem placed me between a rock and a rock, feeling like if I breathe too hard I'll make a costly mistake.

I felt imprisoned by the decisions I'd made that tanked, along with the future I was scared to face that needed me to set boundaries and intentions so I could see progress. I was at the point of accepting the feeling like I didn't deserve better. I remember having to choose between buying lunch… or putting gas in my car. I chose gas. And sat there, hungry, wondering how my life had gotten to that point. Days like this really broke me, leaving me sobbing over the steering wheel, making my Mom Life Crisis that much more difficult and draining. I felt broken – like someone had taken a beautiful vase- my life- and shattered it on the ground. Each time I tried to glue a piece, like a new job prospect, back on, it fell off again. Applying to over 200 jobs and not landing even 10% in interviews really does something to you. At some point, I had to ask myself: What if this isn't failure… What if it's redirection?

I'm so grateful to have worked on my mindset because I still struggle with limiting beliefs and staying focused to make my dreams happen, but shifting my mindset to at least thinking I may be able to accomplish something I wanted, needed or deserved pulls me through. I'm only human, right? Being 'only human' doesn't mean we can't do amazing things. I had to learn to talk to myself like I would to my best friend – with encouragement instead of doubt. That's when I started leaning into something different. My voice. My experiences. My purpose. I stopped asking, "Who will hire me?" And started asking, "What am I called to build?"

I've been working on making my Tasha G. Brand a success and choosing myself. It's been hard being broke, broken, uncomfortable, confused, angry, hurt, ashamed, embarrassed and exhausted for so long. And did I mention, I had become a pro at covering up so my loved ones don't see me suffering. The little girl in me still screams and has tantrums, hoping to be seen, heard and loved by others. The little girl in me still needed healing. But instead of waiting for someone else to give her what she needed... I started giving it to myself. I'm teaching her to sit in her uncomfortable emotions and express how she feels because I'm listening. I'm sharing with her that I've grown into a person that I love very much because I know people can judge me for my choices and actions, but I've always worked to do what was best at that point in time with what I knew.

It's Nothing But Yet for me to make my dream of the Mom Maintenance Community a reality that's needed by so many. The awareness and accountability we need to put us first is a gamechanger because we as moms and caregivers know what it's like to not feel supported or appreciated even when we did everything the "right way". It's time to keep it real and accept that you deserve to be happy in your career/calling. When you find something you like to do, it improves your mood, attitude and overall life and honestly that's your birthright!.

Balance Exercise 3

Rediscovering Your Purpose

1. What work has made you feel most alive?
2. What work has drained you?
3. What did you dream about doing before life got complicated?
4. What's one small step you can take toward that now?

Reflecting on how pursuing something you genuinely care about might change your mood or life. This kind of exercise turns your story of wishing into actionable inspiration for you to course-correct or at least inject passion into your present career situation.

Quick Morning Exercise*: Write an affirmation that counters your biggest limiting belief about your career. If your belief is 'I'll never be successful doing what I love,' flip it: 'I am capable of creating success on my own terms. **(Say it to yourself every morning.)***

This chapter was a wake-up call that a "good job" or a shiny title isn't the same as living out your purpose. You learned that following someone else's definition of success can leave you feeling empty and unfulfilled, especially when you are taking care of a family. But sis, it's never too late to realign your life with what truly lights you up. Let's explore that now. Grab your pen and journal and dig into these prompts to reconnect with your passions and path:

- **Revisit your career choices.** Think back to when you chose your current job or career path. How much of that decision was based on what others (family, society, or even well-meaning mentors) said you "should" do? Write about what **you** originally wanted for yourself versus what you felt pressured to do. How have those choices made you feel about your work and yourself?

- **Envision your dream path.** Imagine you had no fear and no outside pressures – what would you love to do for a career or calling? Write down the dream role, project, or business that excites your soul, even if it feels out of reach right now. Describe why it excites you and how you would feel each day living that reality. (Don't hold back here – let yourself dream on paper, sis!)

- **Plan a small bold step.** Now, think of one small step you can take this week toward that passion or a more fulfilling work life. It could be as simple as researching a class, updating your résumé, reaching out to someone in a field you care about, or setting aside an hour to work on a passion project. Write down the steps you will commit to and when you'll do it. Then journal about how taking this action – honoring your ambitions – makes you feel now, and imagine how your future self will thank you for it.

A "good job" isn't the same as a meaningful life. And success isn't about doing what looks right… It's about doing what feels aligned. It's not too late to choose differently. It's not too late to choose yourself. Sis, keep dreaming and keep taking action – this is how you turn your Mom Life Crisis into your rebirth. Remember, this book is your personal workbook. You can revisit these pages anytime you need inspiration or encouragement to stay on track with building the life you truly want. Every time you come back, you'll see more growth, more strength, and more of you shining through. You've got this!

Now let's talk about the question you've probably been asking this entire time…

Alexa, play Jill Scott Living My Life Like It's Golden!

Chapter 5

Is the Mom Life Crisis Hell?

Is the Mom Life Crisis hell? Honestly… it can feel like it. Like everything is falling apart at the same time. Like you're losing yourself while trying to hold everything else together. But what I've learned is this: It's not the end. It's the beginning of your rebirth. It felt like everything in my life was exploding at once. But instead of destroying me… it forced me to rebuild. And that rebuilding? That's where my power came from. Choosing to live by choice, not by chance feels weird but great! Some of you probably come from the generational epidemic of "What happens in the house stays in the house…" and you are still chained to that fixed mindset. It took me decades to realize that initial seed of fear that was planted in me by relatives left me feeling unworthy of so much because I was not seen, heard or validated in places that represented home and family.

The negative spiral I was in for so long really had me embracing survival mode as a companion when it was really the thief of my joy. I'm grateful for living through my 20s and 30s because I was able to trade in the suffocating M.O.M. mode, the elixir that I drank to induce my Mom Life Crisis, for hope and transformation. Since the age of 40 I've been embracing the idea of transforming because I deserve better, and it's been scary and hard. You know what else has been scary and hard?: not speaking up about my unhappiness in relationships with loved ones, being so indecisive that I've talked myself out of things that were just for me because they were JUST FOR ME, and needing pain in my life for me to be motivated to move forward and embrace progress, especially when it is tied to something that I prayed for!

I'm EXHAUSTED from holding the burden of wanting to be free like it's a curse instead of letting the healing happen as it should; to let myself be wrapped up in the cocoon and have my own damn metamorphosis that I've been training for in the Trauma Olympics. Is the Mom Life Crisis hell? It sure feels like it. But I see it as a purgatory of sorts – a necessary, transformative in-between – certainly not a permanent damnation. In fact, it was the crucible that forged a new me. Your Rebirth is just that: YOUR Rebirth. It's your chance to give yourself the permission to truly break and rebuild. You deserve to become aware of how you've been hanging on by a thread. You've been doing it all even when you have nothing left while promises have been broken to you, leaving you to figure things out amidst the chaotic moments and emotional breakdowns of life. I'm wishing for you to have the same type of breakthroughs I did from doing the work. I'll never forget the day I realized I didn't hate the woman staring back in the mirror. I smiled at her, puffy eyes, flaws and all, and said 'I love you' – and meant it. That's when I knew there was light in that long dark tunnel and I was stepping into that light! I had to take accountability for the ways I avoided my own healing. Not because everything was my fault… but because my growth was my responsibility. I desperately needed a plan, especially for the times when I felt triggered, neglected and abandoned by those I cared for and sometimes even put before myself. The Plan I made for myself is the Plan I want to share here with you because it's time to turn the focus squarely onto you – the author of your own rebirth story.

I knew I needed something structured. Not just motivation… but a plan I could actually follow. That's when I created what I now call the PLAN framework. ***Reflection: Your Nothing But Yet Journal*** is a special section devoted to your growth, a space for you to process everything you've felt and to plan the path forward. Consider this your supportive space, a personal heart-to-heart with your sister-friend (that's me!) as you pour your thoughts onto the page. Get comfy: grab a cup of your favorite tea or a glass of wine, curl up in a luxurious spot, and let's reflect. You've been through a lot, and you've come so far – now you get to gently unpack what it all means for your next chapter.

Think back for a moment on where you started: the overwhelm, the exhaustion, the feeling of being stuck in a Mom Life Crisis that had consumed your identity. You've cried, you've questioned, you've learned to acknowledge the truths you were avoiding. Then you began to find hope – your perspective shifted as you realized you are not alone and that your needs and dreams *do matter*. You've stepped out of survival mode and started daring to envision a life where you thrive. This journal can be your ongoing companion in that journey. Writing is powerful – remember, this very book grew out of my own journal! – and it will help you stay honest and committed to yourself. When you write, you translate the intangible feelings and hopes swirling inside you into concrete words. It's like shining a light in a dark room; suddenly, you can see what's really there and navigate your way through. Use your Nothing But Yet Journal to capture this transformation and keep it going beyond these pages.

Below are some guided journaling prompts and exercises based on the PLAN framework I am introducing. These aren't one-time homework assignments, but tools you can return to whenever you need clarity or encouragement. Take your time with each prompt. There are no right or wrong answers – this is **your** story and you're writing it in real time. Be honest with yourself, be kind to yourself, and don't hold back. This is where the *old you* meets the *new you* on the page and they have a lot to talk about!

Ready? Let's do this.

P — Promise Yourself

What is one promise you are making to yourself?

....

Why does it matter?

....

L — Lay the Foundation

What small actions will support that promise?

....

What habits need to change?

....

A — Align

Who supports your growth?

....

Who drains your energy?

....

N — Never Settle

What will you no longer tolerate?

....

What boundaries will you set?

....

List your *non-negotiables* that honor your worth. For instance, "I deserve to be spoken to with respect, so I will communicate calmly but firmly when someone crosses a line," or "I deserve time to myself, so I will set the boundary that Sunday mornings are for my self-care and I won't make commitments during that time." As you write, notice if a little voice of doubt pops up ("Do I really deserve this?"). If it does, write an answer back to it: *"Yes, I do, and here's why..."* This might feel awkward, but trust me, it's empowering. Finally, write a short manifesto or letter to yourself at the end of this section – a heartfelt promise that you will never again settle for less than you deserve.

You could begin with:

"Dear Self, from this day forward, I promise you will not settle for crumbs, because you deserve the whole damn cake. I will protect you by... (setting boundaries, speaking up, walking away when something isn't right, etc.). I will remember that my worth is not determined by others, but by how I treat myself. You are worthy of love, respect, luxury, joy – and I will make sure you get it. Sincerely, Me."

Make it as poetic or as plain as you like – what matters is that it resonates with your heart. This written commitment is powerful. Whenever you feel tempted to slip back into old habits of settling, come back and read these words. They are your shield and your compass.

Moving Forward: Take a deep breath. Look back at what you've written in each part of your journal reflection. That right there is *your personal PLAN*: your Promise, your Foundation, your Alignments, and your refusal to Never Settle. It's like a loving blueprint drawn by *you*, for *you*. How amazing is that? You've essentially created a self-care and self-growth roadmap that is completely unique to your life. Remember that this journal is a living tool. It doesn't end here. I encourage you to revisit these prompts regularly – maybe every few weeks or months – because as you grow, your answers will evolve. Add new promises and goals as old ones are fulfilled. Check off actions that have become habits and add new actions that you're ready to tackle. Update your support network list as you meet new like-minded souls or deepen relationships with those who lift you higher. Refine your boundaries list as you learn more about what you need (boundaries, like muscles, get stronger with practice!). Let this journal be an ongoing dialogue with yourself.

On the hard days – and yes, they will come, because rebirth doesn't mean life suddenly turns easy – use this journal to ground you.

- When you feel aimless or discouraged, read your original Promise again and remember *why* you started and how far you've come. This is how you nurture the new you: with patience, honesty, and yes, a lot of journal ink.

- When you start to feel lost and unfocused go back to where you wrote about laying your foundation. Review the 2-3 things you wrote here that help motivate the seeds you are planting in your rebirth.

- When you feel lonely or unsupported, flip to your "Align" page and reach out to someone on that list (you wrote those names for a reason – those are your people!).

- When you feel yourself slipping back into people-pleasing, or when doubt creeps in, open up to the "Never Settle" page and remind yourself of the queen you are.

On a more personal note: I am so proud of you. In writing this book and sharing my story, I hoped it would spark something in you – a realization that you're not alone and a resolve that you deserve more. Seeing you here, writing *your* story, is the greatest reward. Your Mom Life Crisis was not an ending; it was a rebirth waiting to happen. Just like a butterfly emerging from a cocoon, you have been through a metamorphosis. It took pain, it took time, and it took courage, but here you are with your beautiful new wings, ready to fly. As you go forth, embrace the fact that you are not your past. You are the author of your future, and every blank page in your Nothing But Yet journey is an opportunity to write that future as boldly and beautifully as you want. Whenever you catch yourself thinking "I can't do this" or "change is too hard," add one tiny word to the end of that thought: *"...yet." I can't do this... yet. I'm not completely healed... yet.* That word "yet" is a promise in itself – a promise that with time, effort, and self-love, you *will* get there. Because *nothing* is fixed in stone, and nothing is beyond your growth.

Keep believing in yourself, keep writing your story, and don't forget that I and your Mom Maintenance Community are cheering you on. And trust me, sis, *the best is yet to come.* You've got this! Embracing your Rebirth is worth every second you put into it, and I want to see you win and succeed. I know the metamorphosis can be tough, but when the cocoon opens, sis, you emerge a butterfly – no longer in survival mode, but flying. Your Mom Life Crisis was never Hell; it was the fire that forges you into something and someone stronger! You've made it this far and I want you to keep going. You might be thinking, "This sounds great, but can I really do it?" I want you to know I asked myself the same question. I was scared – change is scary. But let me remind you: you've made it this far. You've confronted hard truths in these chapters, maybe shed some tears of your own, and you're still here. That means you're ready. So here's another gift to you from me: Your Mom Maintenance Toolkit!

Your Mom Maintenance Toolkit is considered a living entity. It will continue to grow, with me actively adding resources to it as they come across my path. You've already been blessed with my Nothing But Balance bucket exercise and the Rebirth PLAN exercise, which are catalysts for your awareness, accountability and action, but you need and deserve more on your journey. These resources have helped me immensely and I share them so they might light your path as well. As you explore them, remember that your journey is unique – take what resonates and run with it.

These are the tools that helped me rebuild my life:

- Journaling, which turned into this book… (who knows, your story might become a book too!)
- Meditation (start easy by searching simple breathing techniques on YouTube.)
- Music to cry and dance to (I've created my own YouTube Emotional Wellness Playlist which you can access by joining my Mom Maintenance Community. You could also create your

own playlist by saving songs that speak to your heart, mind and emotions.)

- Therapy (and this time I plan on sticking with it!)

- Walking in my calling as Tasha G. The Transformation Guide (I SWEAR this chose me. I'm just trying to catch up & honor this major life changing role!)

- Breaking those generational curses that have been holding me back like shame and fear. (Talks I've had with moms in the Mom Maintenance Community as well as family members have helped with my healing and acceptance.)

- Researching what childhood wounds have been keeping me stuck (when you are able to call a thing a thing you take some of your power back!) Learning about Childhood Emotional Neglect (CEN) from Dr. Jonice Webb and about Mother Wounds & Father Wounds REALLY opened me up and cut out the cancerous traumas, jumpstarting my healing journey.

Of course you can search on the internet to find information that connects and resonates with you, but I wanted to also share some books that have also helped me through my Rebirth. There's so much to embrace and become aware of that you may read some of these more than once, including my book! As you heal you receive information differently, so keep this list handy to help you when you need it.

Book Club List

- ***Dr. Jonice Webb- Running On Empty*- helped me understand and process Childhood Emotional Neglect.

- ***Mel Robbins- The High 5 Habit*** and ***The Let Them Theory*-** The High 5 Habit helped me start with a simple way to take positive actions in my day that empowered me. The Let Them Theory helped me to see where I was stuck in my survival mode controlling ways. The awareness gave me the freedom I've been seeking.

- *Paula Swope- Thought Snob-* Shifted my mindset to see that I'd been thinking too small about my self worth and it was time to step it UP!

- *Rachael Rodgers- We Should All Be Millionaires-* taught me to embrace a wealth mindset as a woman with big dreams for my calling

- *Dr. Joe Dispenza- Breaking The Habit of Being Yourself-* helped me take accountability for holding myself back with old habits and beliefs

- *Princella Clark- The Game- 41 Shades of Men-* put me on to the REAL about men, their nature and thought process when it comes to life

- *Gay Hendricks- The Big Leap-* Opened my mind to see I deserved better in life just because I was born

- *Kelly McDaniel- Mother Hunger-* helped me understand the Mother Wound and how it impacted my life in so many ways

- *Iyanla Vanzant- Peace From Broken Pieces-* a story of empowerment that inspired me through tough times on my journey as a woman

Being reborn is harder than your initial birth because you are starting over from experience and that can be hard with all of the hurt, pain and confusion that is taking up space in your life. For some of you choosing yourself is difficult because you feel like no one else has ever done that for you… until now. It's a different kind of pain when neglect & abuse have been doubling down on you for so long. Finally being able to see light at the end of the tunnel after you've settled for being a People Pleasing Pushover for so long can be jarring but such a relief. You are not your past and it is time for you to think about what you really want for yourself. How do you balance the buckets in your life so you can feel fulfilled? And how can you manage your emotions in an empowering way?

I'd love to hear about your rebirth. Connect with me on Epic, TikTok and YouTube or join our Mom Maintenance Community on Discord or the Skool Community to share your story and find your tribe. Remember how I thought I'd never survive 2020? I did – and so will you through whatever you're facing. You're a badass mother and an incredible woman; don't you forget it!

Repeat after me: *I am not my past.* I am not the mistakes, the traumas, the labels. I am a possibility! I am *Nothing But Yet* – My story is still unfolding, and this ending is really a new chapter beginning!

Now it's your turn… Your Mom Life Crisis has been your call to action. Now I invite you to answer it.

Using the journaling prompts we worked on together as reference:

- Create a small action plan (even 3 bullet points) for the next month incorporating what you learned
- maybe a boundary you'll set…
- a self-care routine you'll start…
- a goal you'll revive...

This is your PLAN for rebirth; keep it somewhere visible.

Remember, you are not alone. Share your journey – tell a sister-friend about what you've learned, or connect with our community of moms on the Rebirth path. We're stronger together: Join the Mom Maintenance Community online!

- Keep this book as a workbook – revisit the exercises, scribble in the margins, make it a living document of your growth

It's Nothing But Yet for you, me, all of us – our past is not our finale. It's time to step into the Golden Girl Era- living life on your own terms and finding happiness along the way. Your rebirth is waiting. Go forth, my friend, and claim it.

Alexa, play Happy by Pharrell!

I love you and want you to remember to Be Well!

Xoxo- Tasha G.

BONUS! Your Rebirth PLAN Journal

A Personal Invitation from Tasha G.

Sis,

You've made it this far — through the chaos, the breakdowns, the quiet tears, and the tough questions. You've confronted your "Mom Life Crisis" and said:" I want more… I deserve more… and I'm transforming because I deserve better!"

This is your space. Be honest. Be real. This is where your transformation begins. Use these pages freely. Scribble in the margins. Let your breakthroughs spill onto the page.

Because your story? It's *Nothing But Yet.*

Be Well,

Tasha G.

How to Use This Journal

This section builds on the **PLAN** framework from the book:

- **P** – Promise yourself 1 thing and stick to it.
- **L** – Lay the foundation for your Promise to make it happen.
- **A** – Align with like-minded people to help you remain focused with your promise.
- **N** – Never settle because you deserve the best, so set boundaries and honor them.

Each part includes:

- A short reflection
- Journaling space
- Encouraging reminders

P – Promise Yourself One Thing and Stick to It

Reflection Prompt:

What is one bold, loving promise you are making to yourself today?
Why is this promise important to your healing and happiness?

My Promise to Myself:

....
....
....
....
....

Mini Action:

What will help you keep this promise when things get hard?

☐ A reminder in my calendar

☐ Saying "no" more often

☐ Asking for support

I will honor this promise by:

....
....
....
....

L – Lay the Foundation for Your Promise

Reflection Prompt:

What do I need emotionally, spiritually, or logistically to stay grounded in this promise?

Supportive habits, tools, or routines I want to start:

....
....
....
....
....

3 Things That Can Support My Promise:

1. ....
2. ....
3. ....

This week, I will commit to:

....
....
....
....

A – Align with Like-Minded People

Reflection Prompt:

Who reflects the energy I need to grow and stay focused?

My Aligned Circle:

-
-
-

How these people support me:

How can I connect with them more intentionally?

What boundary might I need with someone who drains me?

N – Never Settle. Set Boundaries and Honor Them.

Reflection Prompt:

Where in my life am I settling or shrinking?

Boundary I need to set:

....
....
....

How I will protect this boundary:

....
....
....

Anchor phrase to remember when I feel tempted to give in:

....
....
....

Your Ongoing Promise

Remember, Sis — this book is not a one-time read. It's your **personal workbook**. Revisit these pages as often as needed. Reflect. Recalibrate. Reinvent. Choosing yourself isn't easy. It's uncomfortable. It's emotional. It will challenge everything you've been taught. But it is necessary. Because the version of you that you're becoming? She's waiting on you to show up. Take one step this month. Set one boundary. Start one habit. Choose yourself— just once. That's how everything changes. You are not your past. You are not your mistakes. You are not what you've been through. You are who you choose to become next. This is your rebirth. This is your moment. And your story?

It's Nothing But Yet.

About the Author

Tasha G. is a mindset and wellness coach, author, and advocate for women navigating emotional healing and personal transformation. Through her own journey of overcoming childhood emotional neglect, relationship challenges, and the pressures of motherhood, she has dedicated her life to helping other women reclaim their voice, rebuild their confidence, and prioritize their well-being.

Her work focuses on emotional awareness, boundary setting, and guiding women out of survival mode into intentional living. Nothing But Yet is her powerful debut, offering both a personal testimony and a practical roadmap for women ready to turn their breaking point into a rebirth.

www.ingramcontent.com/pod-product-compliance
Lightning Source LLC
Chambersburg PA
CBHW071327030726
47594CB00002B/566